A Cup with Rumi

TO

_____

FROM

_____

Praise for Flamur Vehapi's
A Cup with Rumi

"Once again, Flamur's new book of poems is an inspiration for people of all backgrounds. These beautiful poems are full of life lessons and reminders about the past and the future ahead of us."

—**NASER BRESA**, author of Retrospektiva

"Vehapi's collection of poetry is fascinating and keeps the reader engaged throughout.... A great book to share with friends and family."

—**ROBERT HARRISON**, author of Britain in the Middle East: 1619–1971, and professor, Southern Oregon University

"These are poems of deep thought and reflection, intertwined with motivational wisdom from the spiritual realm."

—**BURHAN ALDIN FILI**, author of
You Were Created to Be a Star, Not a Burning Meteor

"A book full of wisdom and inspirations. I highly recommend it to anyone; whether they are readers of poetry or not, they will simply love it."

—**HATHAL BIN MAQBAL AL SUBAIE**, manager, Culture Center at King Fahd Military Medical Complex, Dhahran

"This precious collection of poetry will soothe the hearts of poetry lovers no matter who or where they might be."

—**DIDMAR FAJA**, author of
Shprehi Dhuntitë E Zotit Tënd

"I found myself compelled, humbled, and charmed by this amazing set of poems. Flamur navigates universal themes with joy, reverence, and humor. It reminded me to go out and do something meaningful with this precious time called life."

—**DANA LUNDELL**, director of mentor programs, University Studies, Portland State University

"Beautiful poems containing a message of love, understanding, and peace, and many other much-needed reminders in a world full of distractions."

—**SALMA AHMAD**, president, Islamic Society of Greater Portland

Also by the Author

The Alchemy of Mind: Poems

Sfidat Jetike: Poems (in Albanian)

Conflict Resolution in Islam: Islamic Approaches to
Peacemaking and Conflict Resolution

A Cup with Rumi

Poems by

Flamur Vehapi

WITH FOUR INTRODUCTORY ESSAYS AND
APPENDICES BY THE AUTHOR

Copyright © 2015 by Flamur Vehapi

All rights reserved. No part of this book may be reproduced or transmitted in any form or by any means, electronic or mechanical, including photocopying, recording, or by any information storage and retrieval system, without written permission from the copyright owner.

Typeset in North by Michaels & Michaels Creative, LLC

Dedication

This book of poems is dedicated to my wonderful wife, Nicole, and my beloved parents, who have always been great supporters of my work. It is also dedicated to my brother and sister and their lovely families.

"You were born with wings,
why prefer to crawl through life?"[1]
—RUMI

Table of Contents

Introduction	i
A Note from the Author	iii
Rumi's Life and Works	vii

PART 1

The State of Human Beings	1
I Know You	5
The Nobody	7
Poet Without Words	9
On Pride	11
The Universe and I	13
Witness to Inhumanity	15
A Story of Life's Destiny	17
A Traveler	19
Looking at You	21
On Love	23

PART 2

Reflections and Remembrance; Forgetfulness and Its Consequences	25
I am Not from Here	29
Days of Remembrance	31
Where to Now?	33
Wishing There Were Words	35
Dust of Ignorance	37
I Am Back	39
Falling in Love	41
Ever Wondered?!	43
Why?	45
The State of the Heart	47

PART 3

A Time for Change; Stepping out of the Illusion	49
A Strange Case	55
Open the Doors	57
A Short Life	59
What We Really Need	61
Time is Running Out	63
Self-Deception	65
The Affairs of People	67
People to People	69
Another Day	71

PART 4

The Need for a New Beginning	73
Mastering Another Art	77
Dust	79
Just a Reminder	81
Conquering the World?	83
Do What Is Expected of You	85
Our Return	87
Soul	89
The Love Advice	91
The Praiseworthy One	93
Chosen	95
Acknowledgments	97
Author's Biography	98
Glossary	99
Appendix A: Selected Qur'anic Verses	102
Appendix B: Selected Hadith	104
Bibliography and Other Suggested Readings	106
Notes	108

Introduction

I am extremely proud to introduce you, the reader, to this fine work of poetry from Flamur Vehapi. I have known Flamur since his days as a student at both Southern Oregon University and Rogue Community College. During his student work in Oregon, Flamur was an exceptional leader with tremendous drive, dedication, and persistence.

This unique work of poetry will allow you to think clearly about our world and the complexities of human kindness, communication, and development. Flamur is an articulate and thoughtful person who has developed keen insights into our world and has become an author exceedingly worthy of our attention and thought.

Please read *A Cup with Rumi* slowly and with a thoughtful, learning attitude. You'll find your outlook expanding with each page. Flamur uses his poetry to take us on a journey; it is an adventure well worth the experience.

Peter Angstadt, PhD
Grants Pass, Oregon
Spring 2015

A Note from the Author

Almost everyone who reads Rumi falls in love with his writings. Simply put, Rumi is not your common poet; he blends beauty, color, and truth through the power of words. Rumi has become a source of inspiration for people of all faiths and even to those who ascribe to no faith. As Jonathan Star writes:

> Nowhere have the impulses of Eastern and Western spirituality been more vividly expressed than in the works of ... Rumi. His poetry is a boundless fusion of all time and cultures.... During his lifetime, Muslims, Jews, and Christians were all inspired by his company and found that his teachings illuminated the spiritual truths of their own faiths. To this day, seven centuries later ... people are still illuminated by his spirit for they can't help but see some aspect of themselves revealed ... or some hidden feeling perfectly expressed.[2]

On the same note, Coleman Barks states:

> Rumi's place in the history of religions is as a bridge between faiths. The story of his funeral in 1273 is well-known. Representatives came from every religion—Muslims, Christians, Jews, Buddhists, Hindus. When questioned about this, they responded, "He deepens us wherever we are."[3]

I was first introduced to Rumi's poetry in 2006 while attending college in Southern Oregon. Knowing I was into poetry, a friend asked if I had read any of Rumi's poems. "Rumi who?" I asked, puzzled. "Rumi, the famous Persian poet," my friend replied. I clearly had no idea who this Rumi was, but now that this strange name had been mentioned, I was compelled to look him up.

That evening, I read biographical notes on Rumi. He undoubtedly had a fascinating life and had written an impressive number of poems and parables, but having been accustomed to a more modern and Western-style poetry, I found his poems difficult to follow, so I set them aside and did not think much more about them for a while. The following year, however, I took a a number of world literature classes taught by one of my favorite professors. I was fascinated to learn what was out there!

In three short terms, I discovered much of the world literature that had been hidden from me due to Kosova's outdated educational system—a system plagued by the propaganda of communism, socialism, and nationalism in former Yugoslavia. Previously, I had never known of the existence of African, Indian, Arabic, Persian, Turkish, or other world literature classics. That is because to many proud communists and nationalists there at the time—heavily influenced by Orientalist rhetoric—people "over there," meaning outside their world, had nothing to offer them. The worldview of nationalists is a very narrow one, I must say.

The great five-century-long Ottoman cultural heritage and influence on the Balkans, for example, has repeatedly been covered up, and attempts have even been made to wipe out awareness of this history, mostly by the last century's nationalists in the region. The empire's significant contributions to the people of the Balkans—whether in infrastructure, architecture, culture, literature, or art—have long been ignored or deliberately denied any connection to the Ottomans. Moreover, in the constantly rewritten versions of history by Balkan nationalists in such countries as Macedonia, Serbia, and Kosova, the Ottomans were in their lands only to seize what was not theirs and oppress, kill, and destroy. Looking at the record of the Ottomans in the Balkans and elsewhere with lenses other than those of the nationalists, however, one sees a very different picture: one of acceptance, tolerance, and a flourishing of civilized culture across many aspects of life. (The Ottomans were simply uninterested in harassing anyone as long as subjects paid their taxes.) To this day, unfortunately, Ottoman contributions to the region remain ignored or discounted by most Balkan peoples.

A poet like Rumi—who wrote of the greatness of God; the inspiring examples of the prophets given to humanity; the parables of love, tolerance, equality, and acceptance of others—has no place in the world of most nationalists. Such literature was suppressed. Needless to say, most of the self-declared "democratic" countries in the region of the Balkans are very cautious of anything that appears religious or even spiritual, to the point of being ashamed of any such connections to their countries or governments. Ironically, some of these governments have gone as far as suppressing by force the voices of their religious populations (whether these populations are a majority or a minority) in the name of democracy, even though their people who put those leaders in power were and are over 90 percent of one religious background or another.

Rumi, however, was included in the world literature books my professor used in our class. He introduced this ancient poet with a video on his life and works. Listening to Coleman Barks reading Rumi's poetry and hearing his comments on the poet's life and works made me rethink my initial judgments about Rumi and his writings. This man clearly had a message to share with the world and a unique talent for expressing it! "No wonder this man is America's bestselling poet today, over seven centuries after his death," I said to myself.[a]

I have been reading Rumi's poetry ever since, and I often find myself inspired to write in response to his lines. Although I am not a mystic myself, I enjoy and admire the way Rumi plays with mystical ideas through poetry. Indeed, I think all poetry is mystical. Certainly Shakespeare's poetry was shrouded in mysticism; we still unpack messages from his works four centuries later. However, having read biographies of Rumi and discussed his life and works with devoted admirers who are native speakers of Rumi's mother tongue, I have learned that Rumi was most definitely not a New Age

---

a. Coleman Barks's *The Essential Rumi*, for example, sold more than 100,000 copies.

kind of person or poet as described by some Western writers today. Moreover, despite the common understanding of Rumi belonging to the Sufi tradition of Islam, some have pointed out that various classical scholars of Islam, including contemporaries of Rumi, have said that Rumi along with his father, son, and grandson were all recognized scholars of the Hanafi school of Islam and that, like his other family members, Rumi was "nothing but an orthodox Sunni scholar," poet, and jurist of the highest caliber.[4]

Rumi is not the only one who inspires readers hundreds of years after his death in a far land; other such eminent figures include Rabia al-Adawiyya, Hafiz, Saadi, and, more recently, Muhammad Iqbal. Unfortunately, many of these great writers have barely made it into the pages of Western books, yet some feel they greatly surpass the writings of numerous Western contemporaries in quality, language, and style. Some Eastern writers like Rumi simply *connect* with us in this day and age, even though they passed away centuries ago. It is this amalgamation of classical beauty and relevance to present-day challenges I address in this book.

The Rumi verses in this book are some of my favorite selections from his works, and I have included in this collection to serve as daily reminders and often as "refreshers" for the reader. My poems, of course, are in no way an attempt to match Rumi's poetry but are instead inspirations drawn from his works and other remarkable poets. The poems within represent my efforts to capture a moment and express the beauty of creation bestowed on us by the One and Supreme Creator of all. However, I do not believe poetry or any sort of writing or speech does justice to that kind of beauty, but I have contemplated and concluded that all I can do is try to do so. I hope you enjoy these humble verses and reflect on them.

Rumi's Life and Works

In the thirteenth century—as the Near East was undergoing struggle and war because of Crusader and Mongol expeditions from both East and West—in the town of Wakhsh, present-day Tajikistan, in September 1207 CE, a natural poet was born. This person was to give a whole new meaning to ancient and even modern poetry. His name was Jalal ad-Din Muhammad Balkhi, later to be known in Persian as Jalal ad-Din Muhammad Rumi and today in the West as Rumi. ("Rumi" was his nickname, meaning someone from Roman Anatolia, or simply "the Roman.")

As Rumi's family decided to move westward from their homeland and later performed the pilgrimage in Makkah, they eventually settled in the Anatolian city of Konya in present-day Turkey. There, Rumi studied under various Muslim scholars of his time, and it was in Konya that he wrote his most esteemed works of Persian literature. The young poet did not stop there. After the death of his father, Bahauddin Walad (himself a Muslim theologian), Rumi began teaching at an Islamic school, where he gained fame and respect for the humble work he performed in service of his community. Biographies on Rumi reveal his deep commitment to his faith. We find numerous accounts in which Rumi "prayed the five daily ritual Islamic prayers, fasted during the month of Ramadan, and did many extended voluntary fasts. And there are many accounts in which he voiced traditional Islamic beliefs on many topics."[5]

Later in life, in the early 1240s, Rumi was introduced to a wandering dervish (a mendicant ascetic) called Shamsuddin of Tabriz,[b] whom he came to admire deeply for his profound

---

b. It has now become apparent that Shamsuddin "was not an illiterate and 'wild' dervish as previously thought by Western scholars, but had a solid Islamic education" and that he "belonged to another major orthodox school of Sunni Islamic law, called Shafi'i" (dar-al-masnavi.org, 2014).

and enlightening knowledge. When Shamsuddin disappeared later in Rumi's life, possibly murdered, Rumi found himself lost without his beloved teacher and friend. After this great loss, writes Coleman Barks, Rumi lived a life of reflection and "tending soul growth" as a result, "leaving us a prodigious legacy."[6] This is when Rumi began to write extensively out of sadness, discovering who he really was and what he had been seeking all his life. As a result of his great awakening, we get some of the best verses of poetry written on paper, all carefully composed by Rumi himself in notable works like the *Masnavi I Ma'navi* (*The Spiritual Couplets*) and verses of poetry like the *Lyrics of Shams of Tabriz*.

Rumi was born at a time when trials and conflict were engulfing the Muslim world, including his own birthplace and that of his forefathers, which he had to abandon. Yet, he chose to respond to these life tests not with aggression but by trying to find a common ground between people of all walks of life through his poetry. As one scholar writes:

> *Instead of calling to war, raising armies, and recruiting men, Rumi sought a different route. Trying to remind all, that despite our differences, we were created by a single God, of whom our spiritual connectedness with [Him], will affect our unilateral vision of each other, allowing us to accept each other despite the differences. God, after all, created us in a diverse way, and the world can't run but through respect for such diversity.*[7]

Rumi lived most of his life in the Saljuk Sultanate, and that is also where he finally rested. Rumi died in December 1273 in Konya, Turkey, yet his writings seem to have even greater impact today than ever before. In one poem, he states:

> *The day I've died, my pall is moving on—*
> *But do not think my heart is still on earth!*
> *… Don't weep and pity me: "Oh woe, how awful!"*
> *For me this is the time of joyful meeting!*
> *Don't say "Farewell!" when I'm put in the grave—*
> *A curtain is it for eternal bliss.*

> You saw "descending"—now look at the rising!
> Is setting dangerous for sun and moon?
> To you it looks like setting, but it's rising;
> The coffin seems a jail, yet it means freedom.⁸

The recent popularization of Rumi's poetry, however, has "been attained by a number of sacrifices" according to the American Institute of Masnavi Studies. In their words, these sacrifices include:

1. *a lack of accuracy of the meanings of his words and teachings and*
2. *a deliberate minimization and evasion of verses in his poetry that reveal that he was a pious Muslim all his life, and a very devoted follower of the prayerful daily life exemplified by the Prophet Muhammad*⁹

Rumi's work clearly exhibits mystical influences and tendencies, but what is certain is that he has been greatly misinterpreted and misunderstood by the contemporary Western world. Interestingly, he seems to have anticipated this, as he said in an authentic quatrain:

> I am the servant of the Qur'an as long as I have life.
> I am the dust on the path of Muhammad, the Chosen one.
> If anyone quotes anything except this from my sayings,
> I am quit of him and outraged by these words.¹⁰

Some of Rumi's major works include:

- Masnavi I Ma'navi, *meaning the Spiritual Couplets, a six-volume poem regarded by many as the masterpiece of mystical poetry*
- Diwan-e Kabir, *meaning the Great Work, otherwise known as the Diwan-e Shams-e Tabrizi, a collection of couplets and quatrains named after Shams, Rumi's spiritual teacher*[11]
- Fihi Ma Fihi, *meaning In It What Is in It, a collection of talks Rumi gave to his students*
- Majales-e Sab'a, *meaning Seven Session, containing a collection of sermons Rumi gave on the Qur'an, hadith of Prophet Muhammad, and other topics*[12]

PART 1

The State of Human Beings

Regarding the state of human beings, the Prophet of Islam is recorded to have said, "An Arab is no better than a non-Arab. In return, a non-Arab is no better than an Arab. A red raced man was not better than a black one except in piety. Mankind are all Adam's children and Adam was created out of clay."[c] The significance of this *hadith* is unprecedented, especially considering that it was said fourteen centuries ago and still applies to humanity in the twenty-first century.[d] Firstly, it calls for the dismantling of racism by reminding people there is no such a thing as the supremacy of one race over another but that all are equal in the sight of their Creator. If one is better than the other, as the hadith says, it is not because of race, color, or nationality but because of his or her piety as a human being. Secondly, the hadith injunction is important because it reminds people of who they really are and where they came from: "they are all children of Adam and Adam was created from clay." The beauty of this line is it reminds people they have nothing to be proud of because we all came from the same source, Adam, and Adam was created from clay, and clay is the lowest and most insignificant substance imaginable. Given that we all came from clay, what is there to take pride in? There is nothing in our makeup (race, color, or nationality) that justifies a sense of superiority over another.

The idea that people come from clay, as the *hadith* states, in no way means people are worthless. On the contrary, in the teachings of Islam, every human being is unique and gifted

---

c. Hadith in *Sahih al-Bukhari* and *Sahih Muslim*.
d. For more on the Qur'an and the *hadith*, see the appendices at the end of this book.

with *ruh*, the diving spirit[e] before they are even born. As a result, "this combination of a sublime quality [(the *ruh*)] and low substance [(the clay)] makes for the presence of potential extremes in the unique entity of humankind."[13] According to this logic, we are all created equal out of the same source, and it is personal choice that shapes the course of our lives: we can either choose the low path of being ungrateful, proud, and corrupt, or we can rise up and accept our great God-given potential by being humble and grateful to the Creator and caring for His creation.[f] Rumi ponders why, when we were born with wings, we so often choose to "crawl through life." Even though we *know* what we do is not what we really should do, we continue repeating the same mistakes over and over again. Ah, human beings!

---

e. Qur'an 15:29. The term *ruh*—translated as 'spirit,' 'soul,' or 'breath of life'—is used in Islamic literature to refer to the inner divine human nature. See *Qur'anic Concepts of Human Psyche* by Ansari, 1992.

f. Although usually referred to as *He*, Allah/God is without gender in Islam, and the use of the masculine pronoun *He* is merely a result of the limitation of language.

Poems

"Silence is the language of God,
all else is poor translation."[14]
—RUMI

I Know You

You have never seen me,
Nor have I seen you,
Never in my life,
But we are no strangers.

We have met each other
A long time ago,
At a time when even the earth
Was not in place.

We have met each other
At a time before the universe was created;
Yes, we have met each other
The time we were together
As atoms in a dusty cloud
Before the big explosion
Ordered by our Beloved.

I know you,
I even remember you,
Yet, I have never seen you.

Remember?
We are no strangers!

"You're from a country beyond this universe,
yet your best guess is
you're made of earth and ashes.

You engrave this physical image everywhere
as a sign that you've forgotten
where you are from!"[15]

—RUMI

The Nobody

How foolish of me
To think that I
Could sustain on my own!

What an ignorant creature
I was!

I closed my eyes
To the Light,
Confined my heart
From the Truth
That was knocking on my door
Ever since I was born.

How did I dare
To move a step forward,
Or back,
And not acknowledge
The All-Encompassing Mercy
Of the Beloved.

I should never say
"I, myself
Reached where I am"
Without giving any credit
To the Pathfinder
Of the Lost.

Lo, it is time
To stop and reflect!

"There is a link, without asking how, without analogy,
Between the Lord of man and the soul of man."[16]
—RUMI

Poet Without Words

Today,
I am not a poet,
I am taking a break.

Today,
I don't want to write
Because every word
And every sentence I write
Falls short
In trying to describe
The beauties
Of the Most Beautiful One.

Today,
I am not a poet
But a being seized by slumber,
And lost
In the beauty of God.

Someone out there,
Please write down everything!
Write everything down,
And share it with the world,
Because I am speechless,
I have no words.

"The result of my life is contained in but three words:
I was unripe, I ripened, and I was consumed."[17]

—RUMI

On Pride

How proud
Are human beings
When they act
As if they own the world
And everything in it.

Very proud
Are these creatures
Who were honored
By being given the status
Of the human being,
And God's caretakers of Earth
Yet, they are too proud,
Too proud to even utter a few words
Of appreciation and gratitude!

Verily, we all came from Adam,
And Adam was created from dust.

"The idol of your self is the mother of all idols.
The material idol is only a snake;
while the inner idol is a dragon.
It is easy to break an idol,
but to regard the self
as easy to subdue
is a mistake."[18]
—RUMI

The Universe and I

Looking at the vast
And the immeasurable sky,
The sun
That brightens the darkness
Of our galaxy,
The stars and the moon
Above our heads,
I came to realize
How insignificant
We really are.

I look at myself
And realize that all I am
Isn't really much,
Isn't really anything,
Something not even worth mentioning
In relation to the universe!

All I have seen,
Known, and thought
Is nothing at all.
Nothing but a small dot
Born milliseconds ago
That lives now
And will disappear
In a blink of an eye.

Can't you see it?
It is all right in front of you,
You just need to wake up!

"If you could get rid
Of yourself just once,
The secret of secrets
Would open to you.
The face of the unknown,
Hidden beyond the universe
Would appear on the
Mirror of your perception."[19]

—RUMI

Witness to Inhumanity

All these heavenly bodies,
Plants and animals,
And so much more,
Look at us in amazement,
At what we do!

They have all witnessed
So much since our creation,
And now they are taken aback,
In shock!

We have been around
Not for a very long time,
But since the time we came here
Left everyone around us
With no comments.

We have broken hearts and bones,
Injured, destroyed, and took lives,
And as if nothing happened,
We still went to sleep that day!

They have all witnessed
So much since our creation,
And now, no wonder they do not talk!
But of course, is there anything to say?

Is there?!

"O Heart! Until, in this prison of deception,
 you can see the difference between This and That,
For an instant detach from this Well of Tyranny;
 Stand outside."[20]

—RUMI

A Story of Life's Destiny

This was a story
Written millennia ago,
Yet people have the audacity
To completely ignore it,
Or act as if they had written it
And can erase it
Whenever they feel like it.

Well, let them be entertained
For a while because life is short
And if they ignore the truth
It will certainly not ignore them.

Life, a written story, yet to be lived.
Life, a written story, yet to be told!

> "If thou fleest with the hope of peace and comfort,
> From that side thou shalt be afflicted with misfortune.
> There is no treasure without wild beasts and traps,
> There is no peace except in the spiritual retreat of God."[21]
>
> —RUMI

A Traveler

You, dear one,
Do not depend much on me,
I am only a human
Who happened to stop by here.

Instead put all your trust
In the Unfailing One,
The Lord of Majesty and Generosity.

I am just a poor traveler
Who is lost in this ocean
Of love.

"Birdsong
bring relief
to my longing
I am just as ecstatic as they are
but with nothing to say.
Please, universal soul,
Practice some song
or something,
through me."[22]

—RUMI

Looking at You

The sun is bright
And beautiful,
But if you keep looking at it
It blinds you.
That is how it is
When I look at you.

But I just can't help it
So I still keep looking.

Ah, marriage is such a great gift!

"You are more precious than both heaven and earth;
You know not your own worth."[23]

—RUMI

On Love

The words of the poet are worthless
When attempting to describe you,
They weigh or mean nothing
To this heart that has seen your light
And has fallen in love with it.

Any word, any phrase, in any language
That I can speak
Does no justice
When attempting to describe
What is in this heart!
How can I go on
Dropping words on paper
When no word or verse
Can even get close
To what the eye has seen
And been blinded by!

For now, I will let the heart speak,
And next time I see you,
Please remember
To give me my sight back!
Not so that I can enjoy the world,
But so that I can look at you
Even if it is just one more time!

"Love is that flame which, when it blazes up, burns away everything except the Everlasting Beloved."[24]

—RUMI

PART 2

Reflections and Remembrance;
Forgetfulness and Its Consequences

People have the tendency to forget. They not only forget about their daily dealings, but they also forget to remember their own Creator (some, for one reason or another, have completely taken that Creator out of their lives). This human weakness, as it is described by many religious scholars, has made many to even forget their purpose of life, and this is why there is much confusion in the world today.

Interestingly enough, the Arabic root word for the word *insaan*, meaning "human," is the same root for the word "to be forgetful." Not coincidentally, this root word, *nasiya*, is used in the Qur'an to signify humans and their forgetful nature.[25] Even Adam, the Prophet of God, forgot after he was specifically told not to eat from the forbidden tree, says the Qur'an (20:115). And the worst form of forgetfulness is man's forgetting of his own self "and not recalling why he was created," writes Professor Alaaddin Başar.

Greed and meanness are examples of other such weaknesses. People are mean to each other and are never satisfied with what they have. Concerning this matter a hadith says, "If man had a valley full of gold, he would like a second valley full of gold."[g] (Haven't we met quite a few people who perfectly fit this profile?)

After greed and meanness, another weakness, according to Başar, is the hastiness of human beings. The Qur'an says "man

---
g. Hadith in *Sahih Muslim*.

is given to hastiness."ʰ Başar says that in this state of hastiness man wants to attain his goals in a matter of minutes, but "you need patience and perseverance for this world. The ultimate reality is not the happiness of this world but the prosperity of the Hereafter."[26]

The next weakness mentioned is man's desire to be praised. According to Başar, however, man has little responsibility for the success he has achieved because all he has achieved is by the will and grace of God, adding that in fact, man is created to praise God, not himself.

The other two weaknesses of human beings are negligence and finding excuses. It is said that people have the tendency to avoid service to humanity out of negligence, yet everyone seems to desire a share of the reward without having worked for it.[27] As for excuses, it is no secret that people are full of them.

Yet all of these weaknesses, says Başar, "are essential to man's spiritual progress," adding that without such weaknesses there would be no struggle for self-improvement and the betterment of society. When there is no struggle, there is no progress. In conclusion, he says, "Those weaknesses can be overcome because Allah does not place a burden on anyone greater than one can bear," as it is stated in the Qur'an (2:286).[28] This is why Rumi wrote: "Why should I stay at the bottom of a well, when a strong rope is in my hand?"[29]

---

h. See Qur'an, 17:11.

Poems

"If you are irritated by every rub,
how will your mirror be polished?"[30]
—RUMI

I Am Not from Here

"I am not from the East,
Nor from the West,"
Said our poet friend,
Who is now long gone
With time.

I am here today
To talk to you for a minute,
And drink a cup of tea
Together under the shade
Of a clear sky.

I am here to share my love
With you and those like you
For a day or so.

But remember, very soon
I will be gone too;
Just like everyone else
I will be dust
That the wind will blow away.

My body will taste the earth,
The air, and ocean waters,
It will dissolve
Into bits and pieces
Until The Day comes,
When I wake up
And come together
In front of the Beloved
To speak for my worldly deeds,
For my worldly past,
Which is nothing more

Than a short dream
In a restless night.

I am not of this world
Nor of this life;
I am all over the universe,
That belongs only
To the Giver of Life.

> "All day I think about it, then at night I say it.
> Where did I come from,
> and what am I supposed to be doing?
> I have no idea.
> My soul is from elsewhere,
> I'm sure of that,
> and I intend to end up there."[31]
> —RUMI

Days of Remembrance

When was the last time,
When I was given abundance,
And lifted my hands
And said "thank you"
To the Giver of all?

When was the last time
I stopped and contemplated
Realizing that I was nothing,
Had nothing,
And am nothing?

When was the last time
I stopped and cried
For the love of the Beloved?

When?
I just don't remember!

"Your depression is connected to your insolence and refusal to praise."[32]

—RUMI

Where to Now?

Son of Adam
Where are you going?
How far do you think
You can run away like this?

Do you even know
When you will stop running
From your own destiny?

Adam lived a thousand years
Minus forty,
And at the end
He too had to embrace death.

Son of Adam
Did you forget that your death
Is closer to you
Than your own jugular vein?

Son of Adam,
When you exhale your last breath,
Do you wonder where to then?

"You know the value of every article of merchandise, but if you don't know the value of your own soul, it's all foolishness."[33]

—RUMI

Wishing There Were Words

There are times when I think
Who am I fooling but myself
In trying to describe
The excellence of the Divine.

There is no ink, there is no paper
To write about the bounties
Of the Beloved!
Even if the oceans became ink
And all the wood
Turned into pen and paper
They would not be enough,
And I would run out of words
Trying to describe
The endless beauties
Of the Sublime One.

I catch myself now,
Writing,
But who am I fooling
Besides myself!

"You wander from room to room
Hunting for the diamond necklace
That is already around your neck!"[34]
—RUMI

Dust of Ignorance

None can see the Light
Until the dust of ignorance
Has settled down.

None will see the Light
Until they themselves
At least try to settle down
The dust of their own ignorance.

And certainly,
None can change the state
Of a people
Until they themselves
Try to change it first.

Let us all try
To gather our senses,
Use our heads,
And think!

"If in the darkness of ignorance,
you don't recognize a person's true nature,
look to see whom he has chosen for his leader."[35]

—RUMI

I Am Back

Tempests of the past,
Destroyers of order
In the land of the One, Almighty,
You thought you had killed me,
But I am back.

You thought you had silenced me
Once and for all
When you exiled me from my nest,
Scattered my family,
And burned my humble home.

You thought you had burned my roots,
And poisoned my leafs and fruits,
But I am back.

I am back, not to get my revenge
But to forgive you.

I am back.

> "They say love opens a door
> from one heart to another;
> But if there is no wall
> how can there be a door?"[36]
>
> —RUMI

Falling in Love

Seeing you
Was as if I had seen
All the beauties of the world,
Therefore, I gave all the credit
To you!
But now I know,
I was a bit hasty.

When I saw your charm,
I should have fallen in love first
With the Giver of Beauty,
As a sign of appreciation and awe,
For the One who created you
And all that beauty
That He bestowed upon you!

Now we both know
The right thing to do
Since everything else,
And every beauty
Fades away,
Except one,
And that is the beauty
Of The Only One!

As for us,
We were just meant
To be together,
In love,

Alhamdulilah.

> "What is the heart?
> It is not human, and it is not imaginary.
> I call it you."[37]
> —RUMI

Ever Wondered?!

There is no atom
wandering aimlessly,

There is no cell
Moving around
Without a purpose,

There is no fallen leaf
Without a destination,

There is no being
Created without a reason.

They all have a job to do,
Serving day and night,
And at the end of the day
They will all gather
In front of the Creator of all.

We depend on our Creator,
And He depends on nothing,
He depends on no one.

Ever wondered
Why you are here?

"I closed my mouth
and spoke to you
in a hundred silent ways."[38]
—RUMI

Why?

The longer I live
The more I realize
How cold,
Uncaring and ignorant
Of each other
We have become.

I just wonder
What the observers,
The sun, the moon, and the stars,
Would say about us!

Well, no wonder
They are speechless.

"Looking up gives light,
although at first it makes you dizzy."[39]
—RUMI

The State of the Heart

The heart,
Only a piece of flesh
Caged by ribs
In a dark place
Hidden from the world,
Yet it sees so much
Says so much,
And feels beyond words.

Oh heart, poor heart,
Learn patience
Be what you were created to be
Not what others wish you to be,
For verily, if you are corrupt,
This whole body of mine will be corrupted.

Learn the art of patience,
And be mindful of right and wrong
Because when you and I become dust
And then are called to account
I do not want us to be from those
Who will be disappointed!

I seek refuge in the Fashioner of Forms
From a heart that is not conscious of Him!

"No prayer is complete without presence."[40]
—RUMI

PART 3

A Time for Change;
Stepping out of the Illusion

Islam, as evidenced in the Qur'an and the hadith, encourages reflecting on our lives, studying, using our time wisely, and being productive members of society. Today, however, it seems that many people live a life of heedlessness, disorientation, and idleness with no apparent purpose. They are distracted by the things they surround themselves with. Many of them, for instance, allow media to guide their lives. It is especially saddening to see so many young people waste their lives doing absolutely nothing. Many of these individuals have fallen into an abyss that seems extremely difficult to escape. They live in a world of dreams and illusion; for them, ordinary reality is antiquated and "uncool." A great number of these children is obsessed with videogames, music, movies, drinking, parties, drugs, and other trivialities. Life for them seems to be all about "having fun," and they only live for the present, without even considering tomorrow when in fact they are supposed to be our hope for the future.

These kids are ready to do anything and spend every dollar they can get their hands on in pursuit of fun and time with their friends. This is undoubtedly a global trend. Speaking of American teenagers alone, in one of his documentaries, Douglas Rushkoff points out that in one year alone, "at 32 million strong ... teens spent more than $100 billion themselves and pushed their parents to spend another $50 billion on top of that. They have more money and more say over how they'll spend it than ever before."[41] Clearly, these adolescents live in world of dreams in which they are guided by desire and a wantonness that is drilled into their heads daily by the power of the media.

According to Hamza Yusuf, a prominent American scholar, this kind of wantonness is a disease of the heart "to which the world's affluent societies are particularly vulnerable," adding that:

> Images of wantonness are ubiquitous in our times. Even as one drives, he or she is accosted by billboard advertisements that show the faces of wantonness, people in ecstatic postures and exaggerated smiles and gaping mouths—showing off their supreme happiness because they own a kind of car or smoke a certain brand of cigarettes or guzzle a special brand of beer—alcohol that destroys lives and minds. It is part of advertising theory that when people are constantly exposed to such images, they not only incline toward the product but desire the culture associated with it.[42]

According to Yusuf, "Advertisers sell a lifestyle that glorifies wantonness." This deludes people's minds into making them believe life is all about what they see in advertisements rather than about being happy with what they have. This disease of delusion is certainly not confined to young generations alone. Many adults suffer from it as well.

Even though children are prone to wasteful spending, the blame for this cannot be put on them alone. This is a much larger issue that not only encompasses marketing corporations and TV commercials geared toward making profits but also parents and even entire societies. Understandably, many parents today are faced with numerous challenges—financial problems being one of those even though most of these breadwinners are often overworked—but they are the ones responsible for their children's actions, whether they are conscious of the fact or not. It is the parents' responsibility to be aware of what their children do, watch, eat, and drink as well as where they go and whom they see. Parents are the "skeleton" of their children. If parental support is weak or nonexistent, children rarely succeed in becoming independent because they have no guiding model to follow. Consequently, today's children often end up on the streets with the wrong people involved in reprehensible activities.

We have to examine our problems from every angle because people—especially children—are more complex than we think. Why is this so important? Parents need to stop shirking their responsibilities and start owning up to their parental duties. When the storm of life hits home, it will be too late for them to ask questions such as, "What did I do wrong?" or "Why my child?" Their negligence will be to blame for their own disillusionment.

I remember having a discussion about parenting in one of my psychology classes in college. A classmate said, "As soon as my kids are able to walk and talk, they should be on their own. I am not going to tell them what to do. I don't need to impose my ideas on them." Hearing this, in spite of my natural timidity, I felt obliged to raise my hand and respond. I told the class I had to disagree with my classmate because if she was not going to educate her children and leave them to fend for themselves at an early age without any guidelines, then the street would inevitably end up educating them. I concluded by emphasizing to my peers that "you all know how the streets educate them!" (The professor teaching the course came up to me after class and thanked me for my reply, saying, "Knowing your cultural background, I was hoping you would say that, and you did.")

If we really want a better society, change has to start with us. If we take the first step, our kids will start to follow the people they identify as their role models. Otherwise, if we leave it up to the children themselves to make important decisions and the media to shape their value systems, we will be in big trouble; unfortunately, this is what we are witnessing at present in society. After all, most advertising corporations are in business to make a profit, not to educate our children. So we as parents must be acutely aware and critical of how we raise our children. In fact, we have to do a lot more than our own parents did for us twenty or thirty years ago because they did not face the same challenges confronting us today.

In summary, the global community evolving before us is full of users, takers, and abusers. We must therefore cultivate in our homes and societies more responsible givers, makers, and caretakers. This, and by working together responsibly, is the only way we can survive the tests of time, *inshaAllah*. The following poems, and many others throughout this book, reflect some of the aforementioned challenges humanity is facing today.

Poems

"I have lived on the lip of insanity, wanting to know reasons, knocking on a door. It opens. I've been knocking from the inside!"[43]

—RUMI

A Strange Case

Strange is the case
Of our brothers and sisters,
They walk the earth
As if they own it all,
Every inch of it!

But what do they really own?
Their wealth? Their home?
Or even their clothes?
Their own body? Or their soul?

Ah, none of those,
Only if they gave it a thought,
They would clearly see
That they really own nothing
And I mean nothing at all!

They leave this world
Just as they entered it
Decades ago,
Naked,
With not even a piece of cloth
To cover their private parts.

Welcome to the world;
Hope you at least made preparations
For your journey to leave it
Either today, or tomorrow.

"Die now, die now, in this Love die;
when you have died in this Love, you will all receive new life ...
Die now, die now, and break away from this carnal soul,
for this carnal soul is as a chain and you are as a prisoner."[44]

—RUMI

Open the Doors

It has been a while
Since we closed our doors
To the freedom of mind,

And unfortunately,
Those doors are jammed now,
Rust-covered,
That is why
We are bound to the past,
Unaware of the present,
And the future, for some,
Seems way too far away.

How do you think Solomon
Was able to hear plants speak
And understand animals talk?
It wasn't because he was superhuman
But because he achieved freedom
Of soul and mind.

He understood
That he was nature
And nature was him.

How did he subdue the winds?!
It wasn't because of his force
But because of his peace
In his heart,
That he found
With the Peace Maker,
Creator of all!

What do your doors look like?
I am still looking for mine!

"Knock,
And He'll open the door
Vanish,
And He'll make you shine like the sun
Fall,
And He'll raise you to the heavens
Become nothing,
And He'll turn you into everything."[45]

—RUMI

A Short Life

Many have walked this earth,
But are now long gone,
And what did they take with them?
Themselves and their deeds
Of this world.

And maybe a piece
Of burial cloth, too!

You go crawling
After positions and power,
And the wealth of this world,
Not knowing that such riches
Are only a prison.

When emperors, sultans, and kings
Who owned half of their known world
Weren't able to take anything with them,
What makes you think you will?

Stop running
After the odds and ends
Of this life
Because there will come a day
When none of it
Will come to use,
Except for your good deeds.

"You wander from room to room
Hunting for the diamond necklace
That is already around your neck!"[46]
—RUMI

What We Really Need

Things have filled our closets
And crowded our rooms,
They have made it difficult
For us to breathe
In our own homes,
Yet we keep buying.

They are suffocating us,
Yet we never stop buying
More and more,
Here and there,
And everything,
From everywhere.

What we really need
Is not more things,
But to find meaning
And contentment
With what we have.

Dear friend,
What you want is not what you need,
And what you need is not more things.

Today,
Our world is in no need
Of wanters and needers,
But it is in desperate need
Of thankers and appreciators,
Of givers, and not takers.

"Be empty of worrying.
Think of who created thought!
Why do you stay in prison
when the door is so wide open?
Move outside the tangle of fear-thinking.
Live in silence."[47]

—RUMI

Time Is Running Out

I have all this time
But I cannot
Wake up one day
And realize
That I had
All that time
But I did not
Do anything with it.

I cannot let myself
Wake up one day
And realize
That I had all that time
On my hands
Yet, I did not do
anything with it.

The least I can do
Is to stand up for justice;
Speak out against the evils
We see in the world,
As a wise one said:
All it takes for evil to prevail
Is for good people to witness it
And do nothing.[48]

"You surely are not the remedy for what ails me;
What ails poor me is a very, very long story."[49]

—RUMI

Self-Deception

Friends,
Who are you deceiving
When you proclaim enlightenment?
What do you think
You have achieved on your own?

You have achieved nothing,
Nor will you achieve anything
Unless you are given it as a favor
And a trust,
Or after having humbled yourself
To the Bestower of Honor!

Who are you really deceiving?
None but yourself!

Be thankful,
Before everything you now have
Has disappeared in a blink of an eye!

"And
He is with you
with you
in your search
when you seek Him
look for Him
in your looking
closer to you
than yourself
to yourself."[50]
—RUMI

The Affairs of People

Strange is the case
Of human beings.

They dwell on weakness
Yet they think they are strong.

They were made out of clay,
Yet they think they are divine.

They are merely people
But many live under the illusion
That they are gods.

They live today,
But don't even think
That they will die tomorrow,
Or the day after tomorrow;
It is the same thing.

What are they really thinking?
Who do they really think they are?
Where do they think they are going?

Wake up!
The earth is dying,
And so are you!

"The gardens may flow with beauty
But let us go to the Gardener Himself."[51]
—RUMI

People to People

Never have we learned
From our history,
Not a single lesson.

Although we have written
Thousands of books on it.

And I doubt we will ever learn
Anything from it,
Except for how to kill,
Each other.

We talk so much,
But do nothing,
Except for a few
Who have seen the hell
We have created ourselves,
To ourselves.

Congratulations,
You are now being honored
As a war hero
For killing thousands,
And wounding millions
Of others: your brothers and sisters.
What an accomplishment!

Are you done yet?
Because I do not know
What you are going to tell
To your children tomorrow!

"Time bringeth swift to end
The rout men keep;
Death's wolf is nigh to rend
These silly sheep.

See, how in pride they go
With lifted head,
Till Fate with a sudden blow
Smiteth them dead."[52]

—RUMI

Another Day

Another day is born,
That lightens the earth
With its shining beauty.
Another day is born
Where birds go out hungry
And hope to return full.

Another day is born,
And the leaves fall slowly
On this green grass.

Another day is born
Where the world keeps spinning
And life goes on, for many.

Another day is born,
Just like yesterday,
With everything in place,
Except for you
O bringer of glad tidings,
Messenger of God.

Oh, how much we miss thee!

"Since I have heard of the world of Love,
I've spent my life, my heart
And my eyes this way.
I used to think that love
And the beloved are different.
I know they are the same."[53]

—RUMI

PART 4

The Need for a New Beginning

We are all witnessing how the world is currently experiencing a series of extreme changes. Many of these changes appear advantageous for some (or at least that is what they believe), but the long-term consequences of these variations—mainly resulting from human actions—often turn out to be catastrophic. While we impulsively plunder our natural resources, nature retaliates with an array of natural disasters we are powerless to deal with. On a more personal level, as a minority of people continues to accumulate and concentrate wealth, the rest of us keep getting poorer due to the inequalities of the social systems we ourselves have designed. These are just two examples of the reality we are experiencing today. Troubled by the course our world has adopted, Karen Armstrong, the great British author, wrote in one of her works:

> *Perhaps every generation believes that it has reached a turning point of history, but our problems seem particularly intractable and our future increasingly uncertain. Many of our difficulties mask a deeper spiritual crisis.... Sadly, our ability to harm and mutilate one another has kept pace with our extraordinary economic and scientific progress. We seem to lack the wisdom to hold our aggression in check and keep it within safe and appropriate bounds. The explosion of the first atomic bombs over Hiroshima and Nagasaki laid bare the nihilistic self-destruction at the heart of the brilliant achievements of our modern culture. We risk environmental catastrophe because we no longer see the earth as holy but regard it simply as a "resource."*

Realizing the world's desperate need for a paradigm shift in the mentality underlying our actions, Armstrong adds:

> Unless there is some kind of spiritual revolution that can keep abreast of our technological genius, it is unlikely that we will save our planet. A purely rational education will not suffice. We have found to our cost that a great university can exist in the same vicinity as the concentration camp. Auschwitz, Rwanda, Bosnia, and the destruction of the World Trade Center were all dark epiphanies that revealed what can happen when the sense of the sacred inviolability of every single human being has been lost.[54]

Even though there is still hope for our world, and despite the fact that people have previously overcome difficult challenges (although none of the magnitude presently confronting us), the spiritual revolution Armstrong refers to must happen soon—not today or tomorrow—but *now*. If people do not try to find their "inner compass" and re-orient themselves, their character will remain unchanged. No one else is going to do this for them. They must have the courage to do it themselves. This is why the Qur'an says: "Indeed, Allah will not change the condition of a people until they change what is in themselves [their hearts]."[i]

---

i. Qur'an, 13:11.

Poems

"You are not a drop in the ocean.
You are the entire ocean in a drop."[65]
—RUMI

Mastering Another Art

For centuries
We have learned to fight,
And very often
Have been at each other's throats.
Wouldn't you say
It is time to learn to love one another,
Listen and respect?

Far too often
People have taught their children
The art of the sword,
And it is about time
We also teach them
The art of the pen,
Patience and forgiveness,
And why not the art of prayer!

If we have come so far
As to master the art of war,
Why don't we also try
To master the art of peace.

"There is no salvation for the soul
But to fall in Love.
It has to creep and crawl
Among the lovers first.
...
Only from the Heart
Can you reach the sky.
The rose of Glory
Can only be raised in the Heart."[55]

—RUMI

Dust

I am
Nothing more than
Unsettled dust
From the past
Shaped into a human form,
Frozen in time,
And waiting
For the divine breeze
To blow me away
From this world of dust.
And take my inner self
Back to its Creator,
When and only
Its time is up.

But for now,
I am thankful
For being who and what
I am.

"Life/Soul is like a mirror; the body is dust on it.
Beauty in us is not perceived,
for we are under the dust."[56]

—RUMI

Just a Reminder

You are here, and alive,
Enjoying life, and all its bounties,
Often, however, without much gratitude,
Or care for the one next door.

But what you are forgetting is that
You have been knocking
On the door of death
Since the day you were born!

And I am thinking:
Isn't that a great enough reminder
To wake up and start changing now?

"O my Beloved
Take away what I want.
Take away what I do,
Take away everything
That takes me away from you."[57]
—RUMI

Conquering This World?

They have tried
To conquer this world
By swords and arrows,
Cannons and bullets,
Hate and fire,
But none survived
The blows of time.

The only way
To achieve this goal
Is not by force
But by love.

For love is the only battle
That turns bullets into roses.

> "The lion who breaks the enemy's ranks
> is a minor hero
> compared to the lion who overcomes himself."[58]
> —RUMI

Do What Is Expected of You

I now admit
I was ignorant to believe
That it is was Moses
Who split the sea.

No, it wasn't him,
He only moved his staff,
And by doing so
He did his part,
And it was his Creator
Who took care of the rest.

What is expected of you
Is to do your best,
And the Beloved
Will take care of the rest.

"Let us fall in love again
And scatter gold dust all over the world
Let us become a new spring
And feel the breeze drift in the heavens' scent.
Let us dress the earth in green
And like the sap of a young tree
Let the grace from within us sustain us,
Let us carve gems out of our stony hearts
And let them light our path to love.
The glance of love is crystal clear
And we are blessed by its light."[59]

—RUMI

Our Return

O, Sublimely Exalted,
The Generous One,

How could I have run
Away from you
For so long,
Knowing that
Every cell of my body
Is from you.

And every single cell
Will soon return only to you,
The Inheritor of All.

Verily, we belong to the Almighty,
And to Him we all shall return.

"Hide from the strangers, not friends of the inner ring,
Coats are made for winter, not the blooming spring.
If reason joins forces with reason seeking delight,
Light shall prevail and the Path will be bright.
Should desire couple with desire and trade,
Darkness will descend
And the Path shall fade."[60]

—RUMI

Soul

O restless soul,
I know you want to come out,
I know you want to leave this cage
Of flesh and bones,
I know you want to come out
And meet your Creator!

I know you want to go there
Where you originally came from,
You want to go to your Source,
And I even know
That it is better there for you
But you have to stay with me
For a bit longer
Until our time is up
In this world.

But I know that you want to go
And I can't blame you!

"Let's ask God to help us to self-control: for one who lacks it, lacks His Grace."[61]

—RUMI

The Love Advice

The young man,
Who had thought
He had fallen in love
With the girl in the next town
Asked the wise man
"Old man, why is love
So complicated and doubtful
To the point where I
Fear of asking for her hand?
I have been pursuing her for years
But I never had the courage
To ask her, or tell her
About my true love
For her."

The wise man looked at him,
Replying after a brief smile:
"Love itself is not complicated,
To the contrary,
It is you who is making it so
For yourself!
In fact, everything
In this life is simple,
But it is people who complicate things
For themselves.

"That is so because
If there is true love,
There should be no room for fear!
And if there is any fear
Or insecurity,
That is anything but
True love!"

The young man,
Who had thought

He had fallen in love
Was now more confused
Than before!

What did he now do?
Prayed and sought guidance
For a better self,
And a true love.

> "Love is that flame which,
> when it blazes up,
> burns away everything except
> the Everlasting Beloved."[62]
> —RUMI

The Praiseworthy One

Amidst the dunes, in a land
Long forgotten by the world
In the Year of the Elephant
By the decree of his Lord
A praiseworthy one was born.

As an orphan he was raised
And little did he know
How much he would be praised.

At the age of maturity,
Seeking light for his own soul,
The Almighty granted him
The greatest responsibility,
Giving him the final torch
To deliver its light
To the whole of humanity.

This was no easy task
For him or his followers
But he never complained,
And to fulfill his mission
Strong and determined remained.

After years of hardship,
Pressure, hunger, and torture
His message of peace, justice,
And forgiveness was able to capture
Even the hearts of his foes.

From a forgotten land,
With sacrifice and pain,
He came out triumphant.
For who he was
And what he has done,
To his people, he was
And will always remain
The praiseworthy one.

"The proclamation of Heaven hath come,
the physician of lovers
has come,
If thou wishest that he cometh to thee,
become ill, become ill."[63]
—RUMI

Chosen

The Chosen one
The wisest of men
Chosen to lead
Not just me
Or a few others
But the whole world.

It is such a shame
That you are so misunderstood
By so many
And completely ignored
Out of utter ignorance
By others,
What a shame!

They would have certainly learned
A great deal from you
About who they really are,
Their purpose of life,
And the final destination.

What a shame!

But you know what,
O Chosen one,
It is their loss, not yours.
You completed your mission,
And they don't even know theirs.

It would have certainly been
An empty life
Had I not known you!

"That which God said to the rose,
and caused it to laugh in full-blown beauty,
he said it to my heart,
and made it a hundred times more beautiful."[64]

—RUMI

Acknowledgments

Firstly, all praises and thanks are due to the Most Gracious, All-Merciful Creator for enabling me to bring these modest poems to light. Secondly, there are many wonderful people I wish to acknowledge for their great support, such as my family, friends, and mentors. Innumerable thanks to my wife for going over my work and others for their supervision of this book. Heartfelt thanks Tom Pike, Jane Brockman, Mark Stokle, and Linda Barns for proofreading this collection of poems. Also to Burhan Fili, Kanaan Kanaan, Rick Williams, Robert Harrison, John Richards, Harry Anastasiou, Steven Scholl, Didmar Faja, Tahir Kukaj, and B.J. Seda for their invaluable support and friendship. Special thanks to Joel Hayward for gifting me his book *Splitting the Moon*, which greatly inspired my writing, and also to Masud and Salma Ahmad, Abdullah Alkadi, Hon. Joseph and Shirley DioGuardi, Mike and Linda Tresemer, Rania Ayoub, Judith Jensen, Mehmet Yavuz, Philip Randall, Imran Maqbool, Mohammed Rashedi, Mohammed Haque, Carl, Donna, Anne and Richard Offenbacher, Lori and David Sours, Amy Lepon, Bruce Stanbridge, Mary Jane Cedar Face, Melissa L. Michaels, Echo Fields, Ahmed Al Baloushi, Connie Anderson, Fela Winfrey, Kathy Hoxmeier, Carl Christy, Ali and Aziz Govori, and the following families: Brady and Wright, Bresa, Hurd, Chaudhary, Obaidi, Mirza, Jaffar, Rockholt and Manlulu, Petersen, Sumariwallah, Nesimi, Gashi, and more. I also thank Cesar Nascimento for letting me use his picture of the Blue Mosque for the cover of this book. Finally, I am indebted to the translators of the Rumi verses and authors cited in this book because without their works, like many around the world, I would have been ignorant of Rumi's deep wisdom and thought.

Author's Biography

Flamur Vehapi is a writer, researcher, and poet from Kosova, where he was born and later exiled by the brutal Serbian regime in the late 1990s. After moving to the United States, he received his associate's degree from Rogue Community College in Medford, Oregon, and his bachelor's in psychology from Southern Oregon University with a minor in history. In 2013, he received his master's in conflict resolution from Portland State University. Later, he taught both at Rogue Community College and Southern Oregon University, and recently, he has been teaching in the Middle East. Vehapi was a regular contributor to the PSU Chronicles in Portland, Oregon. His books thus far include Sfidat Jetike (The Challenges of Life) published in 2002 in Albanian, and The Alchemy of Mind, published in 2008 in English, both of which are poetry volumes. His most recent work is Conflict Resolution in Islam. Flamur and his wife currently live in Abu Dhabi, UAE.

Glossary

Alhamdulilah: Praise be to God

Allah: the Arabic word for the one and only God used by Muslims and non-Muslim Arabic speakers alike

Caliph/Khalifa: caretaker or vicegerent; successor to the Prophet, leader of the Muslims

Fitrah: the pure and original human nature as created by God

Hadith: a saying or teaching of Prophet Muhammad

Hajj: the Muslim pilgrimage to Makkah; the fifth pillar of Islam

Hijab: a veil or head scarf worn by Muslim women as well as by women of many other faiths

InshaAllah: God willing, or if God wills

Isa/Esa: Jesus, the son of Mary (one of the mighty prophets of Islam)

Islam: religion of the Muslims, literally meaning "submission to the will of God alone"

Makkah: a city in present-day Saudi Arabia containing the Kabbah, the holiest site of Islam, where Muslims, if able, perform their pilgrimage

Muhammad: the Prophet of Islam, preceded by all of the other prophets (known and unknown to us), including Jesus, Moses, Abraham, and Noah

Muslim: a person who submits his or her will to God alone; the one who accepts Islam

Prophet: an individual chosen by God to deliver His message to humanity (in our case, Prophet Muhammad)

Qur'an: the holy scripture of Islam given to Prophet Muhammad by God through His Archangel Gabriel

Ruh: the soul, spirit, or self

Salaam: the Arabic word for *peace* used by Muslims worldwide

Surah: a chapter of the Qur'an (there are 114 chapters in the Noble Qur'an)

Zakah: poor-due, an "alms tax," obligatory on Muslims; one of the five pillars of Islam

Appendices

Appendix A
Selected Qur'anic Verses[66]

Surah (Chapter) 1, Verses 1–7:

Praise be to Allah, Lord of the Worlds,
The Beneficent, the Merciful.
Owner of the Day of Judgment,
Thee (alone) we worship; Thee (alone) we ask for help.
Show us the straight path,
The path of those whom Thou hast favoured. Not (the path) of those
who earn Thine anger nor of those who go astray.

Surah 2, Verse 255:

Allah! There is no God save Him, the Alive, the Eternal.
Neither slumber nor sleep overtaketh Him.
Unto Him belongeth whatsoever is in the heavens and whatsoever is in the earth.
Who is he that intercedeth with Him save by His leave?
He knoweth that which is in front of them and that which is behind them,
while they encompass nothing of His knowledge save what He will.
His throne includeth the heavens and the earth, and He is never weary of preserving them. He is the Sublime, the Tremendous.

Surah 8, Verses 61–62:

And if they incline to peace, incline thou also to it, and trust in Allah.
Lo! He, is the Hearer, the Knower.
And if they would deceive thee, then lo! Allah is Sufficient for thee.
He it is Who supporteth thee with His help and with the believers.

Surah 29, Verse 46:

And argue not with the People of the Scripture unless it be in (a way) that is better,
save with such of them as do wrong; and say:
We believe in that which hath been revealed unto us and revealed unto you;
our God and your God is One, and unto Him we surrender.

Surah 59, Verse 23:

He is Allah, than Whom there is no other God,
the Sovereign Lord, the Holy One, Peace,
the Keeper of Faith, the Guardian, the Majestic,
the Compeller, the Superb. Glorified be Allah
from all that they ascribe as partner (unto Him).

Surah 112:

Say: He is Allah, the One!
Allah, the eternally Besought of all!
He begetteth not nor was begotten.
And there is none comparable unto Him.

Appendix B
Selected Hadith[67]

Whosoever plants a tree and diligently looks after it until it matures and bears fruit is rewarded.

Every religion has a special character; and the characteristic of Islam is modesty.

Do you love God? Love your fellow being first.

No man is a true believer unless he desires for his brother what he desires for himself.

God will not be merciful to those who are not merciful to people.

The servants of God are those who walk the earth in humility.

Kindness is a mark of faith; those without kindness are also without faith.

Have compassion on those who live on earth and He Who is in the Heaven will have compassion on you.

The most excellent jihad is the conquest of one's ego.

Do not be angry.

A strong person is not he who throws his adversaries to the ground. A strong person is the one who contains himself when angry.[68]

Strive always to excel in virtue and truth.

Say what is true, although it may be bitter and displeasing to people.

Doing justice is charity; and assisting a man upon his beast and lifting his baggage is charity, and pure, comforting words are charity ... and removing that which is an inconvenience to wayfarer ... is a charity.

Indeed, an ignorant man who is generous is dearer to God than a worshipper who is miserly.

Feed the hungry and visit the sick, free the captive if he is unjustly confined, and assist the oppressed.

It is better for a leader to make a mistake in forgiving than to make a mistake in punishing.

Seek knowledge from the cradle to the grave.

An hour's contemplation is better than a year's worship.

He who knows himself knows God.

Bibliography and Other Suggested Readings

American Institute of Masnavi Studies. *Dar-Al-Masnavi*. N.p., June 2014. Web. 27 July 2014. http://www.dar-al-masnavi.org/index.html.

Armstrong, Karen. *The Great Transformation* (pp. xi–xii). Knopf, 2006.

Barks, Coleman. *Rumi: The Book of Love*. HarperOne, 2005.

——— . *Rumi: Bridge to the Soul*. HarperCollins, 2007.

——— . *The Essential Rumi – Reissue: New Expanded Edition*. HarperCollins, 1995.

——— . *The Glance* (back cover), Penguin Compass, 1999.

Başar, Alauddin. (2008, December 12). "It is stated in the Holy Quran that man is created weak. What are the main weaknesses of man?" In *Questions on Islam*. Retrieved July 11, 2014, http://www.questionsonislam.com/article/it-stated-holy-qur8217an-man-created-weak-what-are-main-weaknesses-man?page=1.

Chittick, William C., ed. *The Inner Journey*. Morning Light Press, 2007.

Fadiman, James, and Robert Frager, eds. *Essential Sufism*. Harper SanFrancisco, 1997.

Helminski, Camille. *Rumi Daylight: A Daybook of Spiritual Guidance*. Shambhala. 1999.

Houshmand, Zara. "Rumi: Love's Secret." *The Iranian*. N.p., 12 June 2000. Web. 7 Nov. 2013. http://iranian.com/Arts/2000/June/Zara/index2.html.

Lewis, Franklin. *Rumi Past and Present, East and West*. Oneworld Publications, 2008.

Maulana, Jalal al-Din Rumi, and Camille Adams Helminski. *Rumi: Daylight: A Daybook of Spiritual Guidance.* Threshold Books, 1990.

Mawlud, I. Trans. Yusuf, H. *Purification of the Heart.* Starlatch Press, 2005.

Mirbagheri, SM Farid. *War and Peace in Islam: A Critique of Islamic/ist Political Discourses.* Palgrave Macmillan, 2012.

Moerenburg, Ulma. "In Memoriam: Murshida R.W.V. Feyens." Editorial. *Toward the One* 8 (2007): 7+.

Nasr, Seyyed Hossein. *The Garden of Truth.* HarperOne, 2007.

Pickthall, Marmaduke. *The Meaning of the Glorious Quran.* Amana Publications, 1996.

Sacred Sounds. Dir. Carmine Cervi. DVD. Films for the Humanities, 2000.

Sardar, Ziauddin. *What Do Muslims Believe?* Walker & Company, 2007.

Schimmel, Annemarie. *Look! This Is Love: Poems of Rumi.* Shambhala Publications, 1991.

Shah, Idries. *The Way of the Sufi.* Arkana, 1968.

Star, Jonathan, and Shahram Shiva. *A Garden Beyond Paradise.* Theone Press, 2000.

Wilson, Peter Lamborn, and Na r Allāh Pūrjavādī. *The Drunken Universe: An Anthology of Persian Sufi Poetry.* Phanes Press, 1987.

Younas, Ustadh Salman. "What Do Classical Scholars Say About Jalal al-Din al-Rumi?" *SeekersGuidance.* N.p., 26 Apr. 2012. Web. 27 July 2014. http://seekersguidance.org/ans-blog/2012/04/26/what-do-classical-scholars-say-about-jalal-al-din-al-rumi/.

Yusuf, Hamza. *Purification of the Heart.* Starlatch Press, 2005.

Endnotes

1. As quoted in goodreads.com, 2014.
2. Star and Shiva, 2000, p. xi.
3. Barks, 2007, p. 1.
4. Ustadh Younas, in seekersguidance.org, 2012.
5. Dar-al-Masnavi, in dar-al-masnavi.org, 2014.
6. Barks, 2005, p. xxii.
7. Ahmad Kozba, in OnIslam.net, 2015.
8. Schimmel, 1991.
9. Dar-al-Masnavi, in dar-al-masnavi.org, 2014.
10. Dar-al-Masnavi, in dar-al-masnavi.org, 2014.
11. See Lewis, 2008, pp. 306–314.
12. See Lewis, 2008, pp. 292–293.
13. Mirbagheri, 2012, p. 53.
14. As quoted in thinkexist.com, 2014.
15. Barks, 1995, p. 31.
16. Nasr, 2007, p. 104.
17. Nasr, 2007, p. 31.
18. Helminski, 1999, p. 31.
19. Fadiman, 1997, p. 244.
20. Shah, 1968, p. 114.
21. Nasr, 2004, p. 221.
22. *Sacred Sounds*, 2000.
23. Fadiman, 1997, p. 214.
24. Chittick, 2007, p. 268.
25. See Bayyinah Student Dictionary website, 2013.

26. Başar, 2008.
27. Başar, 2008.
28. Başar, 2008.
29. As quoted in quotegarden.com, 2014.
30. As quoted in in goodreads.com, 2015.
31. As quoted in thinkexist.com, 2014.
32. As quoted in brainyquote.com, 2014.
33. As quoted in brainyquote.com, 2015.
34. As quoted in inspirationpeak.com, 2008.
35. As quoted in goodreads.com, 2014.
36. Star and Shiva, 2000, p. 7.
37. Barks, *The Glance* (back cover), 1999.
38 Trans. Houshmand, 2000.
39. As quoted in entheos.com, 2014.
40. As quoted in entheos.com, 2014.
41. *The Merchants of Cool*, DVD, 2001.
42. Yusuf, *Purification of the Heart*, 2005, p. 29.
43. As quoted in quotegarden.com, 2015.
44. Chittick, 2007, p. 55.
45. As quoted in goodreads.com, 2014.
46. As quoted in inspirationpeak.com, 2008.
47. Barks, 1995, p. 3.
48. Attributed to Edmund Burke, the original quote reads, "All that is necessary for the triumph of evil is that good men do nothing."
49. Trans. Houshmand, 2000.
50. Wilson and Pūrjavādī, 1987, p. 105.

51. Chittick, 2007, p. 92.
52. As quoted in poetseers.org, 2002.
53. Fadiman, 1997, p. 124.
54. Armstrong, 2006, pp. xv–xvi.
55. Fadiman, 1997, p. 115.
56. Shah, 1968, p. 117.
57. Star and Shiva, 2000, p. 4.
58. Helminski, 1999, p. 40.
59. Mirbagheri, 2012, p. 176.
60. From the Masnavi. As quoted in Mirbagheri, 2012, p. 46.
61. Helminski, 1999, p. 18.
62. Chittick, 2007, p. 268.
63. Nasr, 2007, p. 118.
64. Chittick, 2007, p. 204.
65. As quoted in goodreads.com, 2014.
66. Excerpts from *The Meanings of the Glorious Quran*. Trans. by M. Pikthall, 1996.
67. Excerpts from *What Do Muslims Believe?* by Sardar, 2007, pp. 119–122, and other sources of hadith such as *Sahih Bukhari* and *Sahih Muslim*.
68. From Muslim Peace Fellowship, 2014, http://mpf21.wordpress.com/islamic-nonviolence/the-prophet-of-peace-fundamental-hadith-for-peacebuilders/.

www.ingramcontent.com/pod-product-compliance
Lightning Source LLC
Chambersburg PA
CBHW022118040426
42450CB00006B/755